thelwell's
BRAT RACE

D1325027

by Norman Thelwell

ANGELS ON HORSEBACK*
THELWELL COUNTRY*
THELWELL IN ORBIT
A LEG AT EACH CORNER*
A PLACE OF YOUR OWN
TOP DOG*
THELWELL'S RIDING ACADEMY*
UP THE GARDEN PATH*
THE COMPLEAT TANGLER*
THELWELL'S BOOK OF LEISURE*
THE EFFLUENT SOCIETY*
PENELOPE*
THREE SHEETS IN THE WIND*
BELT UP*
THIS DESIRABLE PLOT*
THELWELL GOES WEST*

THELWELL'S HORSE BOX*
(containing *A Leg at Each Corner,
Thelwell's Riding Academy, Angels on Horseback*
and *Thelwell Country* paperbacks)
THELWELL'S LAUGHTER CASE*
(containing *The Effluent Society, Belt Up,
Three Sheets in the Wind* and *Top Dog* paperbacks)
THELWELL'S LEISURE CHEST*
(containing *Up the Garden Path, The Compleat Tangler,
Thelwell's Book of Leisure* and *This Desirable Plot* paperbacks)

* these titles are available in paperback

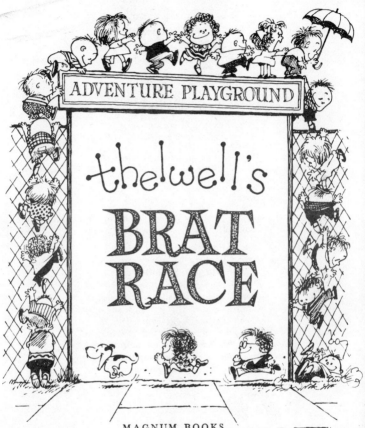

ADVENTURE PLAYGROUND

thelwell's

BRAT RACE

MAGNUM BOOKS
Methuen Paperbacks Ltd

A Magnum Book

THELWELL'S BRAT RACE
ISBN 0 417 01140 7

First published in Great Britain 1977
by Eyre Methuen Ltd
Magnum edition published 1980

Copyright © 1977 by Norman Thelwell

Magnum Books are published by Methuen Paperbacks Ltd
11 New Fetter Lane, London EC4P 4EE

Made and printed in Great Britain by
Richard Clay (The Chaucer Press) Ltd.,
Bungay, Suffolk

CONTENTS

The Little Stranger   7
What's In a Name?   19
The Little Mystics   23
Children's Pets   41
Toys and Presents   61
Children's Ward   81
How to Give a Party   95
Things That Go Bump in the Night   107
How to Keep Them Happy   117

THE LITTLE STRANGER

To most parents the birth of a child is an event that calls for celebration

Few fathers find their offspring very attractive at first

But to their mothers they are the most beautiful creatures on
earth

Correct feeding is of vital importance in the early years –

And he will learn quickly by studying your reactions to his efforts

Babies have a surprisingly strong grip –
which they find difficult to release

They should be talked to on all possible occasions to
increase their vocabulary

There is no need to feel guilty every time your infant misbehaves

But do not base your disciplinary methods on your own
childhood experiences

Remember that what adults may call 'mischief' is merely
the child's effort to acquire new skills

The ability to dress and undress themselves for example is a delight to every youngster

Experts recommend getting them into a playgroup as soon
as possible

*   *   *

WHAT'S IN A NAME ?

Many parents have difficulty in deciding what to call their
baby – here are a few suggestions –

ADAM from the Hebrew meaning FORMED OF THE
EARTH

CONSTANCE
From the French meaning NEVER ENDING

EDWARD
Anglo-Saxon meaning GUARDIAN OF THE TREASURE

ANASTASIA
From the Greek meaning SHE WHO HAS RISEN AGAIN

THE LITTLE MYSTICS

The world-wide fraternity of children is the last and greatest
of the savage, primitive tribes

At first the infant sees his parents as the centre of the universe

But he quickly comes under the influence of a more
formidable power group

They have an exclusive language and folk-lore of their
own and are sticklers for ritual and tradition

Protocol is strictly enforced by the hierarchy –

and punishment for non-conformity is often severe

Children will show enormous courage to gain kudos
within their group

But they are mortally afraid of ridicule

Their games are often primitive

and their songs and rhymes frequently coarse

Their sense of humour has changed little since the dark
ages

It is their nature to be attracted by all that is weird or mysterious

They love to listen to ghoulish and spooky stories

And are full of ancient apprehensions

The school-child grape-vine is staggeringly efficient

– Particularly for rhymes and verses

Which are rarely the ones learned at mother's knee

Most of the traditions are undoubtedly passed on by
grandparents

*　　*　　*

ALFRED
From the Anglo-Saxon meaning ELF'S COUNCILLOR

ANNUNCIATA
From the Latin meaning THE BRINGER OF NEWS

HORTENSE
From the Hebrew meaning ONE WHO COMES FROM
THE GARDEN

HAROLD
From the Norse meaning RULER OF THE ARMY

CHILDREN'S PETS

Many children start by keeping pets which they catch
themselves

They are sometimes introduced into the home without
parents' knowledge –

and housed in unsuitable accommodation

Transport arrangements are often inadequate –

– And feeding methods inappropriate

It is important however to introduce your child to the pleasure of insects and animals as soon as possible

Take him to a good pet shop and let him choose the
animal he would really like to own

– Show him the correct way to handle it –

And make sure that its living quarters are escape proof

Nutritional requirements must be carefully studied

And pets must be visited regularly or they may become
bored

Dogs like to have some corner of the house which they can call their own

Cats tend to vary their sleeping quarters

Some children seem happiest with very small pets –

Others are quite capable of dealing with larger ones

They should be taught the right way to pick up animals

And the correct method of handling fish

Owning a pet gives a child a keen sense of responsibility –

– And a close companionship often develops –

If your child's pet should die – do not try to cover things up

Let him grieve – it is a natural human requirement

PHILIPPA
From the Greek meaning LOVER OF HORSES

GREGORY From the Greek meaning HE WHO IS
ALWAYS WATCHING

RALPH
From the Anglo-Saxon meaning FAMOUS WOLF

GIDEON
From the Hebrew meaning HE WHO CUTS THINGS
DOWN

TOYS AND PRESENTS

Children have very definite opinions on what it is they like to play with

You will notice that it is the simple, adaptable toys like
kitchen junk which children enjoy most

And which encourage both imagination and dexterity

Observe the sort of objects which capture their imagination –

And the kind of games that give them the most pleasure

Do not give them toys which are too expensive to be broken

or which will annoy other people when properly used –

It is a mistake to give presents which you yourself would
like to own –

– Which require expert supervision –

– Or which are unsuitable for the children's age group –

But on no account inhibit their natural curiosity

Presents which give a child a sense of security are always a success

And they adore being given real tools –

Which they quickly learn how to use

Over-complicated games bring about feelings of inadequacy
and frustration

But those that ape adult behaviour are always popular

Remember to test all toys yourself before purchase to make quite sure they are in perfect working order.

*　　　　*　　　　*

MARCUS
From the Latin meaning THE HAMMER

LILITH
From the Assyrian meaning THE GODDESS OF STORMS

BENJAMIN
From the Hebrew meaning SON OF MY RIGHT HAND

CHILDREN'S WARD

If your child must spend a little time in hospital a few of
of his own familiar toys will be a great comfort

There is no need to provide him with special food

Until you have heard the Doctor's opinion on the matter

Some children are a little suspicious of medical examination

Others are more co-operative

Many children adapt quickly to their new situation

and even enjoy the change of routine

Nowadays, creative activity is widely encouraged –

and treatment made as much fun as possible

Highly-trained specialists are quick to diagnose the cause of trouble

And know that the only mildly ill are the most resistant to treatment – and remember what fun it will be –

– The day he comes out

*   *   *

EUSTACE
From the Greek meaning THE GOOD HARVESTER

ANTHONY
From the Latin meaning THE STRONG ONE

PHINEAS
From the Hebrew meaning THE MOUTH OF BRASS

STUART
From the Scottish meaning MINDER OF ANIMALS

HOW TO GIVE A PARTY

Some children run the risk of growing up in social isolation –

The best way to put a stop to this is to give a party

Make sure the children feel personally welcome as soon as they arrive

Move all breakable objects well away from the play area

And never invite more youngsters than you can comfortably
cope with

Children get very preoccupied with the food –

So warn them to leave room for the trifle

Always try to persuade shy children to join in the fun

But play down the prize giving to avoid jealousies

Try to restrict the party to the garden if possible

But if you give a barbecue, fire precautions must be available

Make quite sure the children know when the party's over

*   *   *

THINGS THAT GO BUMP IN THE NIGHT

"Why aren't you asleep, young man?"

Some children can drop off to sleep quickly and easily

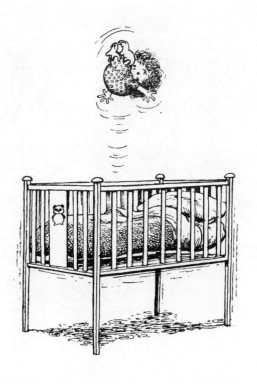

Others seem to find rest impossible

Resistance to bedtime can take many forms

And sometimes becomes a real battle

Some children are simply afraid of the dark

Others are more scared of missing something

Try letting them take a few of their favourite toys to bed –

Or take them into your own bed occasionally – it will do
them no harm

And if they have had a nightmare, always be ready to listen

HOW TO KEEP THEM HAPPY

When children are unable to go out doors to play they
may tend to become a little fractious –

Good parents should be able to cope happily with this situation

Why not teach them how to do spatter work with an old toothbrush?

Finger painting is certain to amuse them

And they will quickly discover the joy of making repeat patterns

Allow them to cut up pictures to make their own puzzles

And do not forget to save your old champagne corks and cocktail sticks – they will need them to make amusing toy hedgehogs

Show them how to blow hen's eggs to make Easter
decorations

And how to make simple patchwork from snips of old cloth

Much amusement may be created by making stilts out of old tin cans

And from simple first aid

Keep a box of old clothes in the lumber room – children
love to dress up

And remember –

Children's play is merely preparation for the harsh realities
of adult life